This big cat is fast, too.

It is called a cheetah.

It runs as fast as a car!

Slow

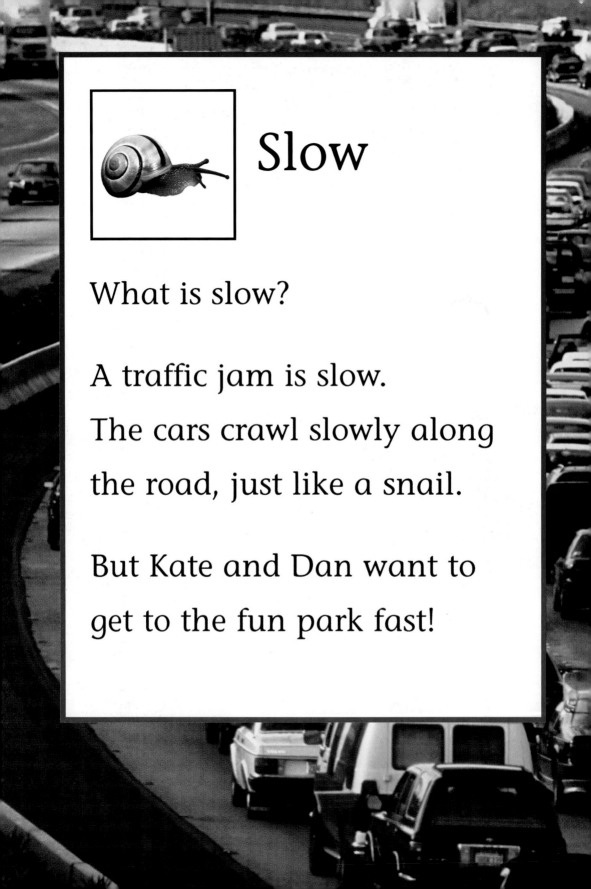

What is slow?

A traffic jam is slow.
The cars crawl slowly along
the road, just like a snail.

But Kate and Dan want to
get to the fun park fast!

Faster

Kate and Dan arrive at the park. They run to the slides.

Kate runs faster than Dan. But Dan is faster than Mum's friend Julie.

Who is faster on the slide?

Dan sits on a mat.

He slides faster than Kate.

He gets to the bottom first.

Slower

Who is slower?

Dan is slower. Kate says he is as slow as a tortoise. But when Kate runs too fast, she falls over.

Sometimes slower is better.

The man on the rope is slow.

If he goes too fast, he will fall off!

Faster and slower

What speeds up?

This ride speeds up!
It goes faster and faster.

Then the ride slows down.

It goes slower and slower.

When it stops, Dan and
Kate get off.

Fastest

Kate and Dan watch the go-karts.

The go-karts go fast.

Mum's kart is the fastest.

It goes like a rocket!

Racing cars are very fast.

They race each other.

The fastest car wins the race.

 # Slowest

Who is the slowest?

Julie is. She takes a very long time to eat her pizza!

A sloth is one of the slowest animals. It can take all day to move along one branch.

 # Spinning

What spins fast?

The seats in this ride spin fast. They go round and round like a top. Dan and Kate get dizzy!

Kate and Dan like to spin fast.

Mum likes the big wheel.

It goes round very slowly.

 # Falling

Then Kate and Dan watch
the air show.

A sky diver jumps from a plane.
He falls faster and faster.

When the parachute opens,
the sky diver slows down.

Slow and fast

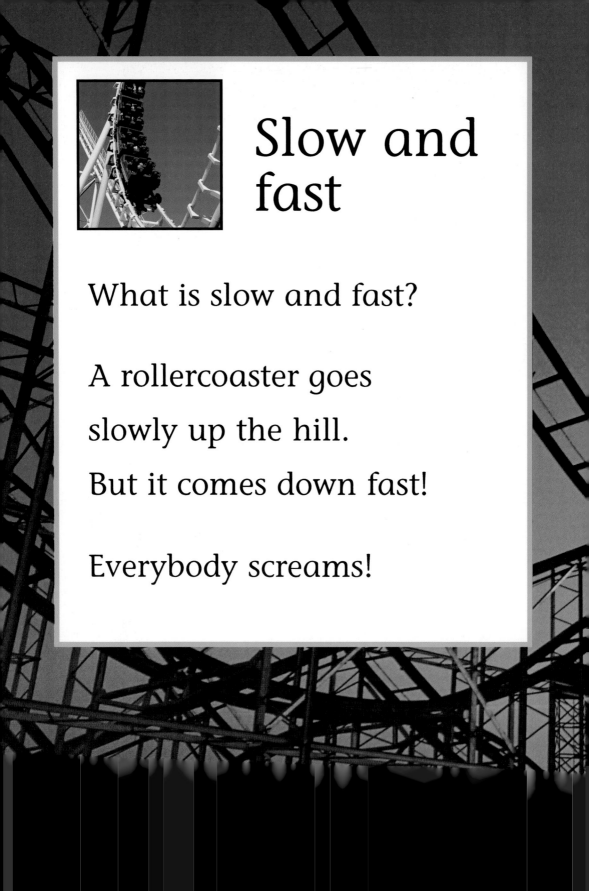

What is slow and fast?

A rollercoaster goes
slowly up the hill.
But it comes down fast!

Everybody screams!

Here are some words about speed.

Slow   Fast

Slower   Faster   Slowest

Fastest

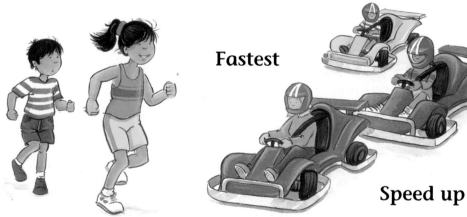

Speed up

Slow down

22

Are these things fast or slow?

Ride

Car

Rocket

Bicycle

Rollercoaster

Can you write a story with these words?

Do you know?
A watch times
how fast
we can run.

A dial tells
us how fast
a car is
going.

Signs tell
people not to
drive too fast.